THE GUITAR STYLE OF
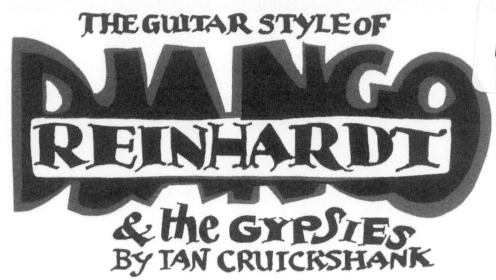
DJANGO
REINHARDT
& the GYPSIES
BY IAN CRUICKSHANK

HAL•LEONARD®

Exclusive Distributors:
Hal Leonard
7777 West Bluemound Road
Milwaukee, WI 53213
Email: info@halleonard.com

Hal Leonard Europe Limited
42 Wigmore Street
Marylebone, London, W1U 2RN
Email: info@halleonardeurope.com

Hal Leonard Australia Pty. Ltd.
4 Lentara Court
Cheltenham, Victoria, 3192 Australia
Email: info@halleonard.com.au

Ian Cruickshank started playing the guitar on a serious basis in 1965 when he formed an R. & B. Group. This lasted until 1969 when he joined the Keef Hartley Band as featured lead guitarist, made two albums (Half Breed and Battle of N.W.6), and toured extensively in England and the Continent. After two years he gave up touring to concentrate on teaching and session work. In 1978 he formed the group Swing Guitars, primarily in order to play the music of Django Reinhardt. In conjunction with fellow guitarist, Trevor Davies, he has made many 'field' trips to France to photograph and record the gypsy jazz musicians, and in 1981 they made a 40 minute movie documentary called "Gypsy Jazz".

Ian is also involved in promoting various gypsy groups and in January, 1981, brought Raphael Fays and his trio to play at the Pizza Express in London. **His present quartet is also called "Gypsy Jazz".**

The purpose of this book is to provide some pointers towards the gypsy jazz style as pioneered by Django Reinhardt, and continued today by many gypsy guitarists. The key to individual progress along this path is relentless application and experimentation, coupled with an intense study of all available information, both aural and visual.

Regarding Django's recordings, one may find several versions of the same tune — each providing (upon close examination) a wealth of information on which to build a repertoire of ideas. Gradually, and in direct proportion to the learning effort put in, the determined student will find the structures, chords and harmonic concept becoming 'second nature'.

Therefore, while learning directly by attempting to play Django's solos note for note has its obvious advantages, the important thing is to emulate the spirit in which this music is created, using the gypsy approach to chords and timing.

Ian Cruickshank

All photographs by Ian Cruickshank © 1982, except photographs of Django, used by arrangement with Max Jones. Photograph of Bireli page 14 by Ian Smith

I am indebted to Dave Bennett for his ideas, practical help and not least of all, his lettering, in the preparation of this second edition.

Ian Cruickshank 1985
31 Grimmer Way
Woodcote
Reading
Berks

DJANGO REINHARDT

Django was born on 23rd January, 1910, at Liverchies in Belgium. He was a true gypsy of the Manouche tribe who were renowned for their creative and entertaining skills. Django spent his early years travelling by caravan around Europe and North Africa and finally settled just outside Paris. Django had virtually no formal education and by the time he was twelve, his overwhelming interest was music and he'd started to play a banjo-guitar as well as dabbling with the violin. By the following year he was already playing in the many cafes and nightspots of Paris, mainly backing accordianists and violinists. The music at this time consisted mostly of waltzes and tangos, plus a few gypsy pieces, all of which Django played with incredible flair to the extent that everybody who heard him was amazed at his dexterity.

The first recordings that Django made were done in March, 1928, backing an accordianist and a slide-whistle player. On November 2nd in the same year, Django returned to his caravan after playing in Paris and either dropped a lighted candle or a match, with the result that the whole caravan was burnt to the ground and Django was left with such severe burns to his right leg and left hand that there was talk of amputation. However, through help from a gypsy doctor and amazing determination on Django's part, he was fully recovered after a period of some 18 months. However, the accident had resulted in the 3rd and 4th fingers of Django's left hand being deformed and virtually useless.

Despite this terrible handicap, Django persevered and evolved a unique guitar style, using mainly two fingers. He would take his caravan along the south coast of France and he and his brother, Joseph, would play duets in the bars and cafes. About this time he was discovered by one Emile Savitry who was a jazz fan with a good collection of records. So it was that Django began to hear people like Louis Armstrong, Duke Ellington and Joe Venuti, and he wasted no time in assimilating jazz into his own playing. Possessing, like many gypsies, a photographic memory, Django would hear a tune once and play it on his guitar five minutes later.

About this time Django met Louis Vola, a French double-bassist, who had his own group and the two of them would play together whenever Django was in the vicinity. Meanwhile, Django's fame was spreading and he made all sorts of recordings with singers and orchestras but, as yet, no jazz. Around late 1933, Django started to frequent a club in Paris called the Hot Club of France which had been started by Charles Delauney and others in order to promote the new 'hot' jazz. Before long, Django had formed a quintet with his brother on rhythm guitar, a cousin or friend on 2nd rhythm guitar, Louis Vola on the bass and Stephane Grappelli on violin. The Quintet of the Hot Club of France was born and in December, 1934 the first records were made. The group was a tremendous success and made many records and tours up to 1939, when the war came and Stephane and Django went their own ways. Grappelli stayed in England, where the Quintet had been touring, while Django returned to France to form another group — this time with clarinet, drums, one rhythm guitar and bass. This continued to 1948 but although Stephane and Django had reunited immediately after the war and were to do so on and off until 1950, Django was by now interested in different forms of jazz, particularly bebop which he had heard while playing in America with Duke Ellington in 1946.

Django became more and more a recluse, feeling that his music was misunderstood and that people only wanted to hear the old Quintet style. He rented a house in Samois, 30 miles south of Paris, and spent his time fishing, painting and playing billiards. He made a few sporadic tours and occasionally played in the jazz clubs of Paris, making his last recording with a modern group in March, 1953. On May 15th of that year, Django set out from his house in Samois for a beer and a game of billiards when he suffered a brain haemorrage. It was a Saturday, and there was no doctor immediately available. Eventually, he was taken to a hospital in Fontainebleu where he died in the night. The world had lost not only the greatest guitarist but a fantastic composer. Fortunately, this illiterate, unpredictable, mysterious gypsy made over 850 separate recordings during his incredibly varied musical career and his playing continues to delight and astound many thousands of fans, old and new.

Django in 1947, playing a Gibson guitar, acquired during his American Tour with Duke Ellington the previous year.

GUITAR-DJANGO style

For any guitarist wishing to study Django's playing methods, the problems may seem, to say the least, baffling. Immediately one is dealing with a musician of formidable stature and a completely unorthodox style of playing which stemmed partly from his physical limitations (the third and fourth fingers on his fretting hand were deformed and could not be used in the usual way) but also from his unschooled gypsy origins.

In this book I hope to provide an alternative approach which will dispense with the need to unravel the various solo transcriptions that are available on the market. While some of these are excellent, they require a high standard of reading and the chord symbols are not always accurate. In conjunction with this book, the most direct ways of learning are through the study of Django's records and, if possible, hearing in person some of the guitarists who are playing in this style today, e.g. Diz Dizley, Raphael Fays, W.A.S.O., the gypsy group from Belgium, and Bireli Lagrene.

The first essential is, of course, the instrument which should be an acoustic guitar with a bright attacking sound, ideally a Maccaferri type like the mass production C.S.L. or better still, a hand made job from a 'good luthier'. The strings should be light gauge and the plectrum a thick rigid type, preferably made from tortoiseshell.

I would recommend the following as being competent makers of this type of guitar:

John le Voi — 8 Hamilton Road, Alford, Lincs. LN13 9HD. Tel: 05212 3341

Jean Pierre Favino — 9 rue de Clignancourt, Barbes, Paris, France.

Jean Pierre Favino will not enter into any correspondence and does not speak English, therefore a visit to his workshop and a smattering of French is essential.

Right Hand Exercises

Here are some runs and scales that will help develop the co-ordination between right and left hands. Remember to pick every note, using up and down strokes where indicated, to obtain a balanced run with no weak spots.

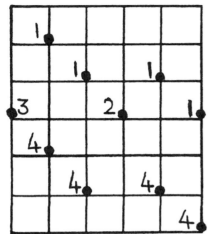

Ascend *from the sixth string to the first using only* **down** *strokes, then play the descending scale starting on the first string using the following picking strokes:-*

∨ ∧ ∨ ∧ ∧ ∨ ∧ ∨ ∧ ∨

DIMINISHED RUN

Run up and down this scale using alternate up and down picking but starting always with a down stroke. Practice this all over the fingerboard from any note to its octave.

Strive to cultivate a supple right hand technique which moves primarily from the wrist, positioning the hand so that it does not rest on the strings or soundboard and with the thumb running on a parallel plane with the strings.

SEMITONE SCALE

This is a favourite device used by Django. Start on the first string using an up stroke then down strokes on third, second and first strings, immediately sliding the whole chord shape up three frets to start again on the first string with an up stroke, thus repeating the whole procedure.

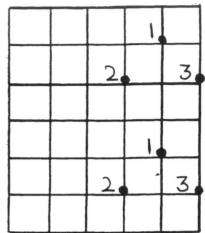

DIMINISHED TRIPLET RUN

By moving this shape up and down the fingerboard at three fret intervals, one is able to give the impression of a continuous line which sounds as though it is being picked with the fingers.

Django often used this device of playing over a chord scale (in this case D6) by first picking the note one semitone below the actual note in the chord.

Start on the fourth string at F (sharp) with a down stroke and follow with alternate up and down picking. This also works well over a major or minor chord scale in any inversion or position.

SEMITONE CHORDAL RUN

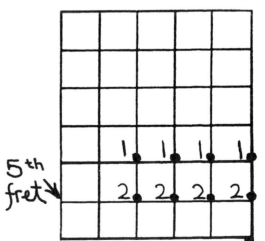

Another good exercise for improving co-ordination is to choose any note on the fingerboard and ascend to its octave on the same string via semi-tones using alternate picking. As with all these exercises the rule is to start slowly and gradually increase your speed, at all times paying attention to tone and accurate co-ordination.

TRIADS, CHORD SHAPES & INVERSIONS

Many of Django's chords were basically triads formed by using only three notes and these were usually played in three main groups, i.e. by using the first, second and third strings, or the second, third and fourth, or the third, fourth and sixth. In the last case the fifth string is deadened by touching it, usually with the finger that is holding down the sixth string, thus allowing the right hand to strike four strings, but sound three. This 'triad' approach has several advantages, e.g. the chords in many cases sound stronger than the corresponding conventional chord where five or six strings are used, also it is good for fast changes and fills so much a feature of the music of the Hot Club. Another beguiling aspect is that these simple three string fingerings can be interchanged so that one shape can "translate" two or three different chords and more if a fourth note is added.

Django would often use his thumb on the sixth string in certain chords, these being marked with a "T" in the diagram. Although unconventional, this thumb technique can be most effective and, in some chord shapes, indispensable. "Ultrafox", from the Ace of Clubs, "Parisian Swing", A.C.L. 1189, provides a good exercise for these lower-string triad movements.

Django & his wife Naguine in London 1946 with a deputation of British guitarists including IVOR MAIRANTS (far left).

ULTRA FOX

Medium Tempo
4/4 Two beats to every chord except where indicated

Numbers at side of chord indicate fret

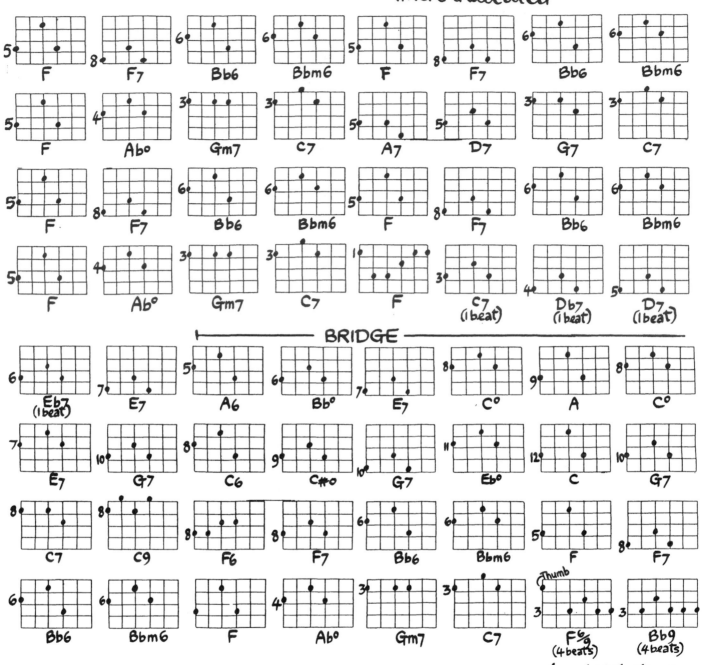

BRIDGE

back to start

TRIADS & INVERSIONS

Here is an example of a twelve bar blues in G. minor using a very simple triad system which occurs, in various forms, on virtually all of Django's minor key recordings. This particular sequence comes from "Blues en Mineur" (Vogue Jazz Legacy series 500100). Although only 2 basic fingering positions are used, they "translate" into several different chords. The fifth string is deadened by touching it with the second finger which is holding down the sixth string. The numbers at the side refer to fret positions. **Play 2 beats to each chord, except where indicated,** *in a medium tempo* $\frac{4}{4}$.

Row 1: 3 — Gm6 | 5 — D7 | 6 — Gm | 5 — D7 | 3 — Gm6 | 5 — D7 | 6 — Gm | 7 — Bo

Row 2: 8 — Cm6 (8 beats) | 6 — Gm | 5 — D7 | 3 — Gm6 | 6 — Eb7 | 5 — D7 | 4 — C#7 | 5 — D7 (4 beats)

Row 3: 3 — Gm6 | 5 — D7 (1 beat) | 8 — Co (1 beat) | 6 — Gm | 5 — D7 | 3 — Gm6

Triads like these are especially convenient and effective in medium or fast tunes. Get a friend to play the chords or record yourself, then experiment with solo lines and arpeggios based on the scales of Gm — B° — Cm — F#°. The interesting part is in the linking together of these lines to form phrases. More of this later.

Bireli Lagrene, London 1982

TRIADS & INVERSIONS cont

Django also used triads to great effect when playing a blues in the major key. Here is a sequence in Bb which serves purely as one example of how these triads can be employed. The idea is to introduce as many changes and variations as possible. The F7b5 in the final bar can be played with the thumb on the 6th string.

Fingering for these triads is a matter of personal preference, depending on physical limits of the left hand etc., but in general it is best to let the second finger hold down the sixth string. More complicated chords can be achieved by holding down the second string with the little finger; the idea being to experiment in this direction to see what fits.

BLUES Two beats per chord except where indicated.

Fapy
Lafertin

Bireli
Lagrene

Movement Within Chords

When Django used triads on the top three strings and on the second, third and fourth strings, he often combined them with a continuous fast strum from the right hand of varying intensity. This gives an impression of a string or brass section, especially when certain notes in the chord are sharpened or flattened or extra notes added, creating movements within the chord. The technique is similar to shaking out a lighted match, but much faster.

The following exercise is taken from the second section of Django's tune "Tears" and can be played either with individual strokes or with the fast strum.

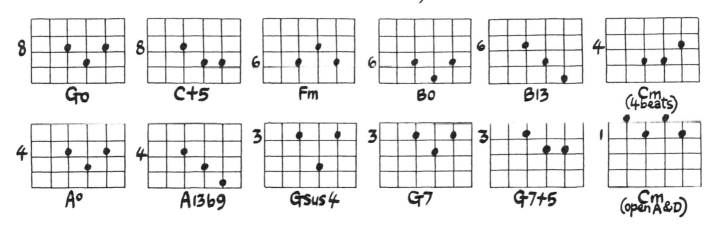

Two beats per chord except where indicated.
Fret number at side of chord.

Django & Les Paul.

ARPEGGIOS

A large percentage of Django's playing contained arpeggio-type runs in various forms and keys. These arpeggios were played usually from a low note to a high note via two, three or sometimes four octaves, resulting in a wide range of the guitar's resonances being sounded almost simultaneously. When in the keys of G or D, Django would often use this trick as an ending.

In these two examples the notes should be played evenly but with a flourish, leaving the last note to ring on. Try to picture the run as one block movement before attempting it at speed. The numbers refer to playing order of notes. In G use only the first and second fingers and the same for D, except the first note is played with the thumb and the last two notes with the third or fourth finger. In both examples pick with down strokes only.

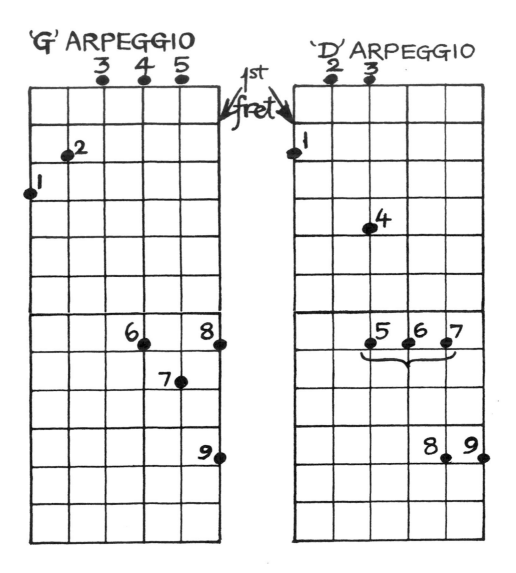

The above examples can be varied in a most effective way by substituting natural harmonics in place of the last note. In G these harmonic notes are found at the 7th or 12th frets and in D at the 7th fret. With the third finger (left hand) barely touch the 1st, 2nd and 3rd strings in a short barre, but instead of holding the strings down, flick your finger away at precisely the moment you strike with the plectrum. If this is your first attempt at harmonics you may find it difficult to synchronize left and right hand movements, but with perseverance it will click.

ARPEGGIOS (cont.)

Here are two examples of arpeggios in F minor which can be used either as endings or as a means of adding texture to a solo. Try them in different keys and always be open to experiment by extending and linking various lines. Again, numbers refer to playing order of notes.

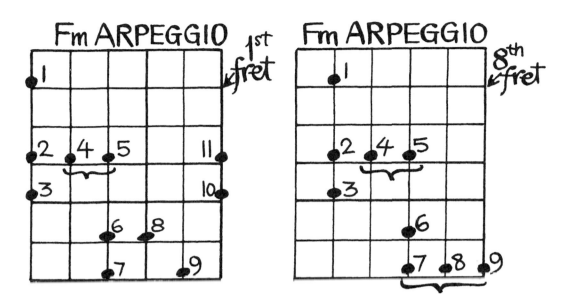

FINGERING 12211332321
PICKING ꟿꟿꟿꟿꟿꟿꟿꟿꟿ

122113333
ꟿꟿꟿꟿꟿꟿꟿꟿ

JOSEPH REINHARDT, SAMOIS 1978

17

Here are four major arpeggios over the chord of Bb which can be played one after the other to create a ripple effect. To get the idea of the timing, think of the phrase, "Jim's a very good boy." Note that the fourth example is an octave above the first. Numbers of the dots indicate playing order of notes.

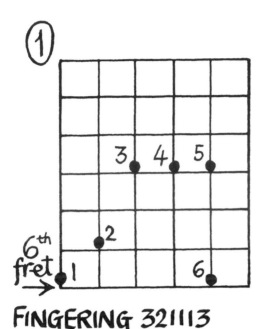

① FINGERING 321113

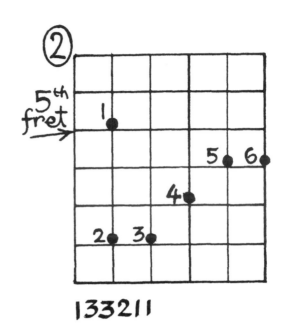

② 133211

Use down strokes only except on the last notes of ① & ④

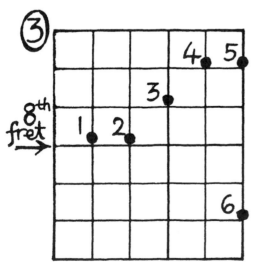

③ FINGERING 332113

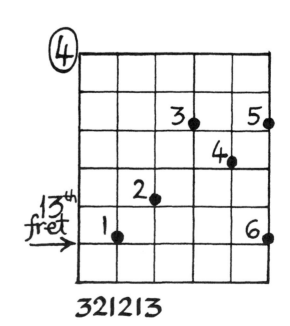

④ 321213

ARPEGGIO in G MAJOR

should be played with 1st and 2nd or 1st and 3rd fingers, using
all **down** *strokes* **except 4th note in Steps (1) (2).**

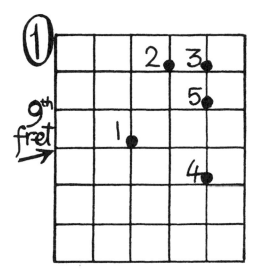

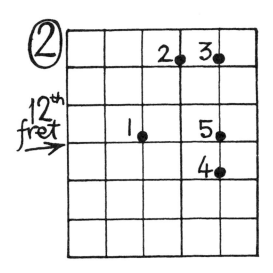

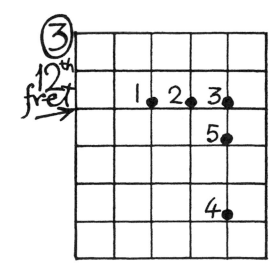

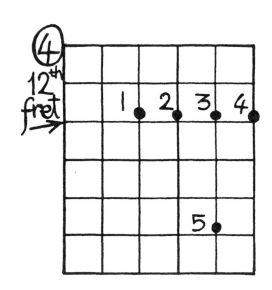

Django's father Jean Weiss ↑

SAMOIS-sur-SEINE
DIMANCHE 21 MAI 1978
25ᵉ ANNIVERSAIRE
de la mort de

DJANGO REINHARDT

10 h   Dépôt de couronnes sur la tombe de Django REINHARDT
11 h   Messe concélébrée par le Père DUBOURG, aumônier régional des tziganes, et l'Abbé IN DEN KLEEF, curé de la commune, avec la participation « des gens du voyage » et autres artistes. Allocution de Monsieur KOSCIUSKO-MORIZET, Ambassadeur de France.
13 h 45 Hommage à Django devant sa maison, 8, rue du Bas-Samois.
14 h   Concert dans l'île du Berceau avec la participation de nombreux artistes.

Spectacle présenté par Maurice CULLAZ, Président de l'Académie du Jazz

avec la participation de :

Joseph REINHARDT · BOULOU et HELIOS · Alby CULLAZ · Louis FAYS
LOUSSON · Louis VOLA · Pierre CULLAZ · Rafaël FAYS
Svend ASMUSSEN · Maurice FERRET · Jo PRIVAT · Jacques MONTAGNE
Bill COLEMAN · Joseph POUVILLE · Charley BAZIN · Maurice VANDER
Bobby FEW · René MAILHES · Pierre LE TAC · René URTREGER
SUGAR BLUE · Georges LOCATELLI · Jean LUDOVIC · Georges ARVANITAS
Hal SINGER · Jean-Paul BERNARD · Jean-Yves LACOMBE · Jean BONAL
Johnny BRITT · Marc BERTEAUX · SERANI · Bob VATEL
Toquinho RAMOS · Christian LETE · Chateo GARCIA · Gilbert LEROUX
MA'Lilet SARRANE · Christian ESCOUDE · Jacques MAILHES

SPECTACLE GRATUIT

↑ Poster for Django Festival 1978

← Joseph Reinhardt (centre) at Samois 1978. On his left is Swedish violinist Svend Asmussen

Samois Sur Seine

MORE ARPEGGIOS

Another way of expanding arpeggios is to run through the related chords in a given key, connecting each line with a link note, resulting in one long ascending line. Here is an example in F utilizing the chord sequence of F — F° — Gm — Ab° — Am — F7. This type of extended arpeggio also works well over the dominant chord of F7 in a tune in the key of Bb, especially where the F7 is held for two bars. For the timing, think of the phrase, "If you ever see a duck," or better still, make up your own!

ASCENDING ARPEGGIO in F

①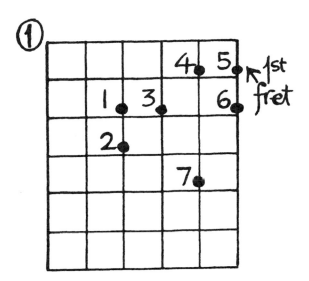

FINGERING: 2321123

②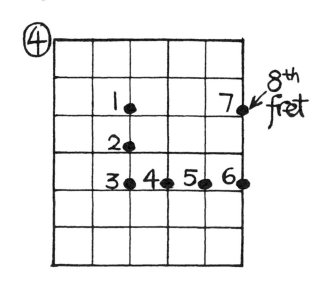

2311123

Use down strokes except on sixth note of
① ② & ③ & last note of ④

③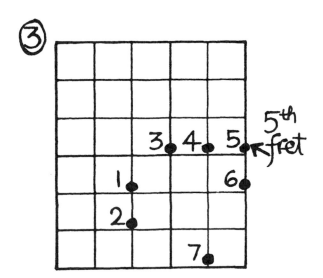

FINGERING: 2311123

④

1233331

OCTAVES

Django made great use of octaves, both in solos and back-up work, in order to underline certain passages or generally beef up the proceedings. How he played them is a mystery, as they require the use of the 1st finger and the 3rd or 4th. Because his 3rd and 4th fingers were crippled, and virtually useless (although he did use them on some chords), he presumably used his first two fingers which entails quite a stretch! Whatever the method, Django was certainly one of the first jazz guitarists to use octaves extensively. Even that most prolific octave player, Wes Montgomery, freely admitted that he got the idea from Reinhardt. Of course, octaves do not occur solely in jazz guitar (both classical and flamenco players, for example, use them), but although most guitarists have some idea of where to find them on the fingerboard, they are frequently neglected as a highly effective means of boosting solos etc.

The octaves Django usually played are found on four pairs of strings, i.e. 6th and 4th, 5th and 3rd, 4th and 2nd, 3rd and 1st as follows:-

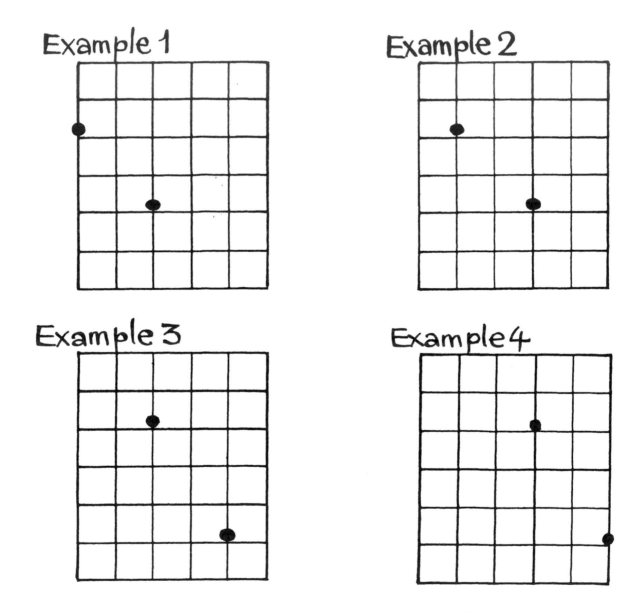

Example 1 Example 2 Example 3 Example 4

Note that the first two pairs (ex. 1 and ex. 2) are played with 1st and 3rd fingers, whereas the last two are played with 1st and 4th fingers. In each case the open string in between is deadened by touching it slightly with the first finger, all three strings being struck simultaneously with the plectrum. Try playing slow, simple melodies or scales using a combination of these octaves and with practice you will build up speed.

Octaves cont.~

Here are two more octaves which are found on the 1st and 4th strings and the 2nd and 5th. Although these are not suitable for the simultaneous damping technique described above, the individual notes can be picked one after the other in quick succession to give a jerky effect. Use 1st and 3rd fingers and move up and down the fingerboard in semitones.

Example 5

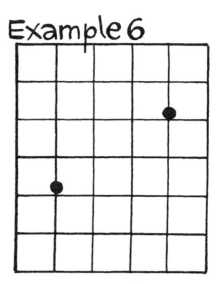

Example 6

Another useful point about octaves is that they provide a good springboard for creating solo lines. For example, supposing you play a line where the last note falls on Bb on the 1st string, you can begin the next phrase with Bb an octave lower on the 3rd string. This gives a nice effect of continuity. Also, you can try this jumping from a note to its octave anywhere in a phrase — for instance, at the beginning, then play a scale relating to the chord sequence which leads back to the original note or any other note in the scale. The main idea, as always, is to experiment all the time as the possibilities are endless.

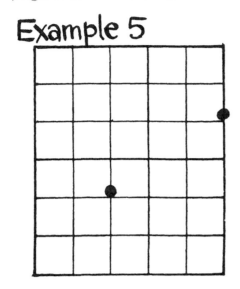

Bireli Lagrene, London 1982

Larry Adler jamming with WASO
l-r Vivi Limberger, Koen de Cauter
Michel Verstraeten (bs) &
Fapy Lafertin

CHORDAL TEXTURES

Django composed many fine melodies, one of the most beautiful being the ballad "Manoir De Mes Reves", also known as "Django Castle". With each recorded version Django finds fresh chordal nuances, as he did with most of his material. A couple of versions are in the key of Eb, but here I've written out the sequence in D, using the more usual chords. Even if you're not familiar with the melody, the chords will suggest it and provide a good example of the kind of close textured harmony found in much of Django's playing. Fret numbers are at the left of each diagram, while the number of beats are indicated below. The first chord of A13 is an introduction and the tune actually starts on the D 6/9. Fingering is left up to the individual but try using the thumb to cover the 6th string, (and sometimes the 5th) in those chords marked with a "T".

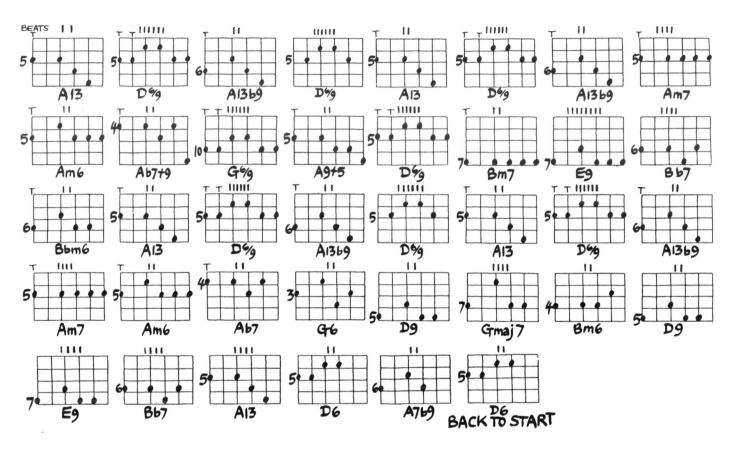

In one version of "Manoir", Django plays the first four bars as follows; leaving the A string to ring on. Suggested fingering is above each diagram.

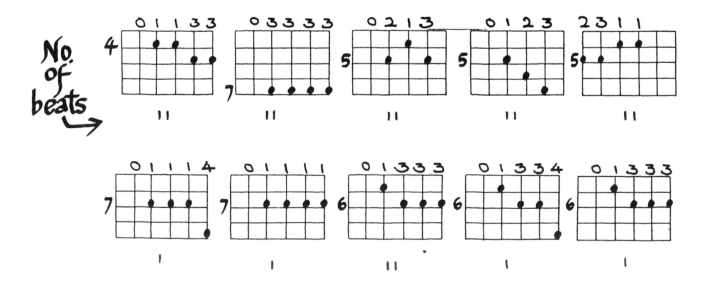

24

CONNECTING SOLO LINES

This could be re-titled "collecting" solo lines, as the art of bringing together what would otherwise be fragmented scales, runs and arpeggios into cohesive expression via one long phrase is a lifetime's study requiring endless experiment. In the meantime, here are examples of three phrases over the chord sequence of (one bar each) Cm7 — F7 — Bb. Notice that diagram (a) when linked with **either** (b), (c) or (d) results in a 26 note phrase which respectively ends on the 5th, 3rd and root notes of the Bb chord.

Diagram (b) involves a C diminished scale over the F7 chord, while diagram (c) uses the same diminished scale combined with a high arpeggio of Cm7. Diagram (d) utilizes an octave jump from the first to the second note and then down in a chromatic, semitone run to Bb.

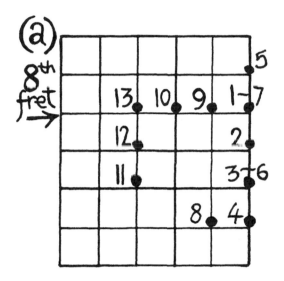

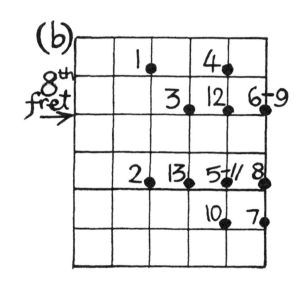

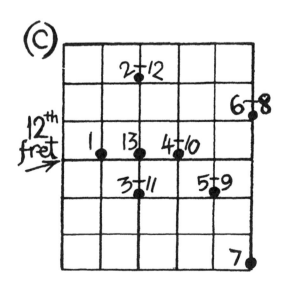

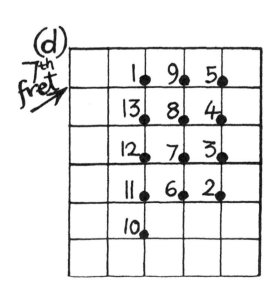

Django, English composer Michael Carr
& Grappelli, pictured before the War.

CONNECTING SOLO LINES cont.~

Here is an example of a series of phrases which, when linked together, form one long line of eighth notes over an eight bar medium tempo 4/4 sequence consisting of the chords C7 — F9 — Bb — G7 — Gm — F7 — Bb. Notice that diagram (d) represents a diminished scale against the G7 chord, also that the last note of diagram (g) has the value of four beats, or one bar, of Bb.

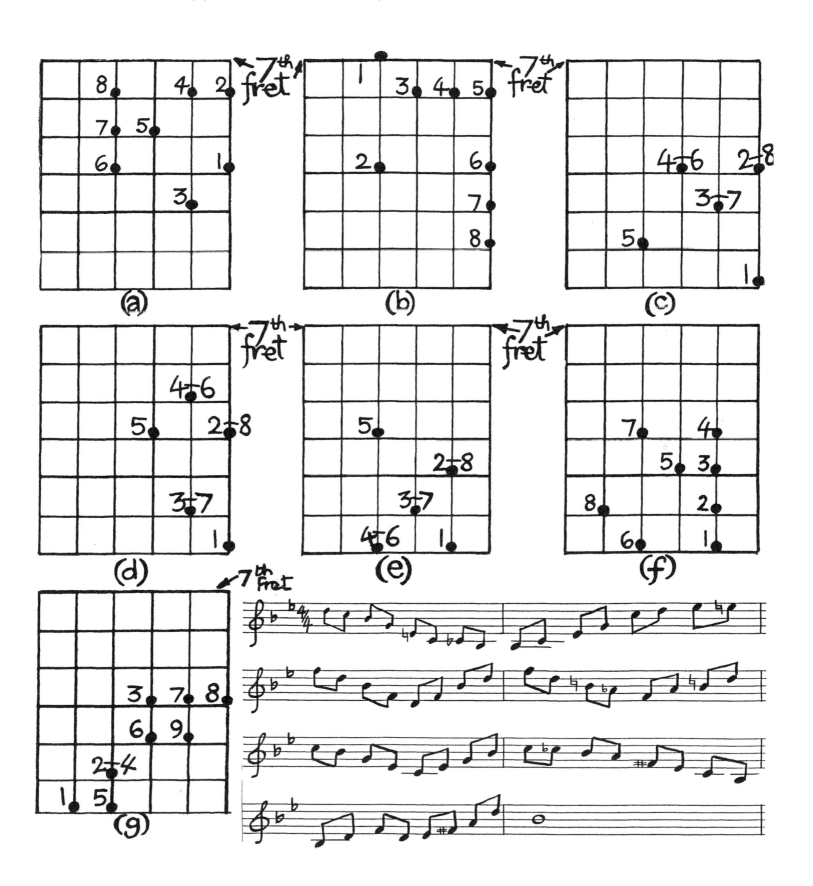

Django
&
Stephane
Nice, 1948

Django & Stephane recording
at Decca Studios, London,
1946

Coleridge Goode (bs)
Jack Llewellyn &
Alan Hodgekiss
(gtrs)

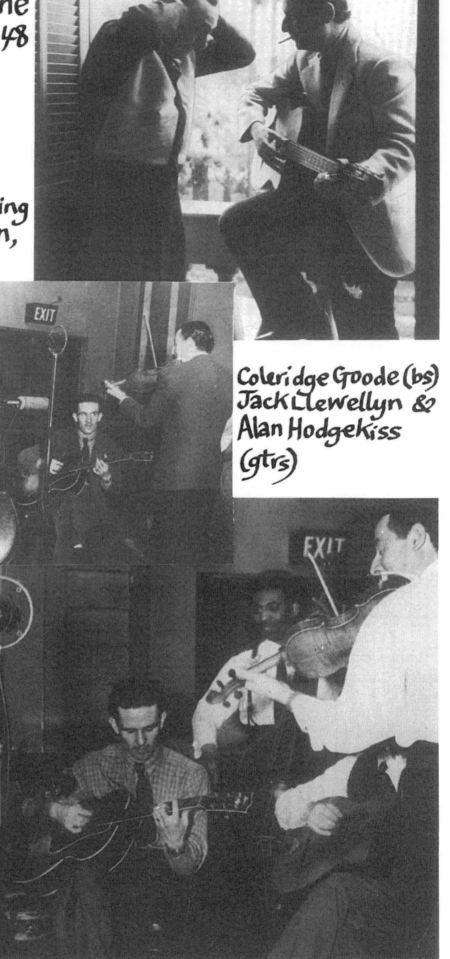

28

TRICKS & DEVICES

Although Django used very few cliches, he nevertheless had certain devices up his sleeve that were guaranteed to raise a few eyebrows. One of the best known of these "trade marks" is the ascending eighth note run, usually over a major scale. Here is an example over four bars in Bb, with an additional phrase leading into Eb. This chord sequence can be thought of as the first part of a standard 12 bar blues with the sequence Bb — Bb — Bb — Bb7 — Eb etc. Use the combination of up and down strokes that feels most comfortable yet ensures that each note is struck clearly.

Note	1	2	3	4	5	6	7	8	9	10	11	12	13	14	15	16
Finger	4	2	1	2	4	2	1	2	2	1	1	2	3	1	1	2

Note	17	18	19	20	21	22	23	24	25	26
Finger	3	2	1	2	3	2	1	2	3	1

Note	27	28	29	30	31	32	33
Finger	2	1	3	2	1	3	1

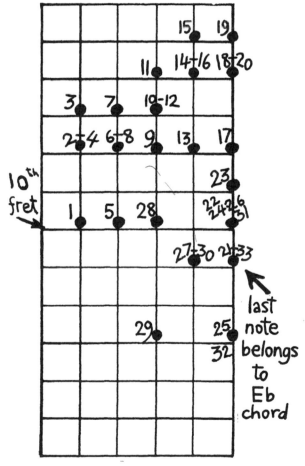

*Exactly how Django fingered this type of run is open to conjecture. Presumably he used his first two fingers, but according to Raphael Fays, Django was able to turn his hand to bring his crippled fingers into play for this particular trick. Try playing it at speed with two fingers and the difficulties are tremendous, even bearing in mind Django's astonishing "two-finger" agility. However, many of Django's lines are, ironically, easier to play with two fingers (after breaking down the mental barrier of having to do everything with three or four). Using only two fingers tends to give the line a bounce that doesn't otherwise occur. It may be said that Django's injuries resulted in a tremendous fingering advantage over conventional players **because** he relied mainly on the hand's two strongest fingers, bringing a special force and consistency of tone to his playing. Also, the fretboard of the guitar somehow becomes more accessible and less 'cluttered' when using two fingers, which, in Django's case, were completely unfettered by the last two fingers being drawn up and back out of the way. This is not to diminish Django's incredible achievement but may explain part of the mystery.*

29

TRICKS & DEVICES *cont:*

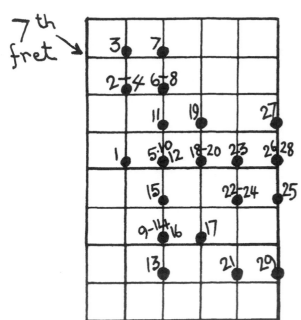

7th fret →

Here is a variation of the previous line. To start with, think in terms of groups of four notes, aiming to strike the first note of each group as quickly as possible after the last note of the preceding group. The best fingering combination is probably found by experiment but it is worthwhile practise to try using only the first and second fingers. As this line is further up the fingerboard some players will actually find it easier to play with just two fingers.

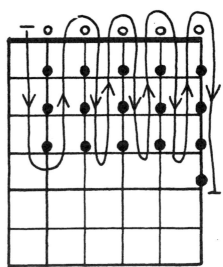

CHROMATIC RUN

Most of Django's famous chromatic runs started with an open string on the bass as shown here. The idea is to think ahead at all times, striking each note clearly with alternative up and down picking. The run shown here goes from bottom A through two octaves to A on the 1st string.

After the open note on each string, use the following fingering in a sliding fashion:-
123 , 123 , 123, 123 , 12222

The run can be extended with the 2nd finger running up to the top A at the 17th fret. Throughout the run, and particularly when working up the 1st string, try to avoid holding the neck of the guitar with the thumb. This will then free the 2nd finger to glide in a co-ordinated way with the right hand picking.

Translating Chord Symbols

Much of the confusion encountered when dealing with chord symbols is due to insufficient knowledge of which shape to play or which inversions and positions blend best with a given melody. Consequently, the student often finds that his interpretation of the chord symbols results in a disjointed progression, sounding only vaguely like the record and involving a great deal of unnecessary left hand movement. Django, due to his physical impediment, evolved a simple but effective way of playing chords and often implied certain notes without actually fingering them. Also, many of his chord sequences have either a built in bass line or an upper line which moves logically through the progression. Sometimes the bass note remains the same for the next chord, becoming a common root for both; likewise, one or more of the upper notes can remain the same while shifting the lower notes. A combination of these techniques, plus a clear, simplified knowledge of inversions, results in a very close blend of sound with the minimum of left hand movement.

Where a major chord symbol is given or heard, it is usually best to play a major 6 or a 6/9, or a variation of these chords. Thus a symbol of F can be translated as any of the following, depending on the melodic context. Fingering is given immediately below each diagram, "T" denoting the thumb and "X" denoting deadened or unsounded strings. The bottom line gives the harmonic relationship, "R" denotes root note. Figures at side are fret positions.

Alternative Forms of F6/9

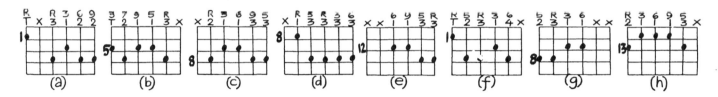

Note that although in the same basic fret position, diagram (f) is a "middle" voicing of (a), (g) is a lower voicing of (c), and (e) is a higher voicing of (h). Below are some useful minor inversions.

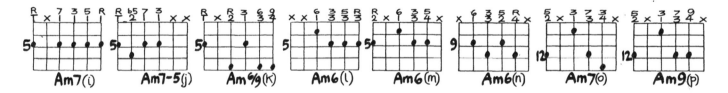

Note how the sound, or voicing, changes in Am6, depending on shape used. Another aspect is that (j) can also be called Cm6, (l), (m) and (n) can be called D9 and (p) can be CMaj7, as follows:

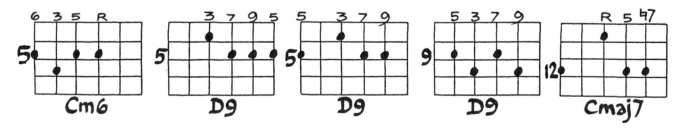

Learning From Records

It is useful to have a record deck that features four speeds, i.e. 16 r.p.m. and 78 r.p.m., as well as the usual 33 r.p.m. and 45 r.p.m. The 78 r.p.m. speed is obviously essential for playing the old "78" records, but it is necessary to have the correct size stylus for this use in order to get the best sound from them. The 16 r.p.m. speed is good for slowing L.P.'s down by approximately half — invaluable when studying fast solo runs. Also the key of the piece being studied remains roughly in the same key (although it is an octave lower) so that retuning of your guitar is kept to a minimum. However, it must be remembered that, for example, what sounds like a sixth string note at this speed is more likely a third string position and so on.

Even if you don't possess one of these older record decks, there is still a vast amount to be picked up by listening to Django's records. The method I use is to first decide on the tune to be studied and proceed to concentrate on it by playing it over as many times as it takes to become aurally familiar with every section. Then take your guitar and determine the key of the piece, bearing in mind all the variables which affect the pitch, e.g. the deck may be running slightly fast or slow or the original recording might similarly be "out" due to transfer from 78 master to L.P. Also, the musicians may be tuned higher or lower than exact concert pitch. All these factors will necessitate re-tuning of the guitar and you will have to decide that if, for instance, the record sounds somewhere between G and Ab or G and F then the correct key is more likely to be G. Although Django was at home in any key, most of his recordings are in the keys of F, G, Bb, Eb, D and C.

Having decided on the key, try working out the basic chord changes without the record by whistling or humming the tune, going back to the record when you get lost. At this point of trying to establish a particular chord it is helpful to listen very hard for the individual components, i.e. the root note (which will usually be on the 5th or 6th string) then the other notes of the chord. Sometimes it is difficult to hear anything except the root and one other note, say the 7th, in which case, experiment by fingering between these two to find the identities of the other notes and then replay the record and compare.

With practice this initially painstaking method becomes easier as your ears become more accustomed to picking out certain notes and disregarding others. By listening to the third string only, for example, you can find out how the chord shapes move. When you have finally worked out the chord sequence you will then have a good basic understanding on which to study the solo lines which are often found around the chords or their inversions and substitutes. This is where 16 r.p.m. comes in, revealing in slow motion the beautiful structures that Django uses and you can often hear a change from one string to another which gives a good indication of the position on the fingerboard.

In short, learning from Django's records requires a great deal of detective work (not to mention patience!) but the results are unfailingly beneficial and so much more direct than studying music theory books. In any one of Django's recordings there is enough learning material to keep the serious student busy for at least 6 months, especially when you consider the different versions that are available, e.g. at least nine versions of Nuages.

RECORDS & BOOKS

Because Django always played with a great deal of spontaneous creativity, all his records are fascinating, but I've concentrated on the more readily available records and literature.

1. EMI/PATHE "DJANGOLOGIE SERIES" 1-20
   THE DEFINITIVE CHRONOLOGICAL SET.
2. DECCA/ECLIPSE TREASURY SERIES
   "SWING 35-39" THE QUINTET OF THE HOT CLUB OF FRANCE.
3. "DJANGOLOGY" VOGUE VJD 5021/2 (2 RECORD SET)
4. BARCLAY 920366 DJANGO REINHARDT
   ET LE QUINTET DE H.C.F.
5. "DJANGO REINHARDT THE VERSATILE GENIUS"
   VOGUE VG405 JLA64.
6. "DJANGO REINHARDT EN BELGIQUE 1942"
   POLYDOR 2344136.
7. THE VERY BEST OF DJANGO REINHARDT FROM SWING TO BOP
   DECCA 6.28441 DP (DOUBLE L.P.)

LITERATURE

1. DJANGO REINHARDT BY CHARLES DELAUNEY
   ASHLEY MARK PUBLISHING.
   The only biography of Django, written by one of the instigators of the Hot Club, jazz critic and entrepreneur, Charles Delauney. Originally published in 1961.

2. JAZZ MASTER SERIES "DJANGO REINHARDT" BY STAN AYEROFF
   MUSIC SALES LTD.
   Examines Django's technique via adapted notation. Accurate and informative for those who read music.

Django's grave, Samois Sur Seine

GYPSY GUITARISTS in the REINHARDT TRADITION

Mainly concentrated in France and Germany there are many gypsy guitarists, each with his own approach but all of them firmly rooted in the Reinhardt tradition. Most of these guitarists have not recorded, and some do not even play in public, but this is no indication of their abilities. The general pattern is that they start playing at an early age and are largely self taught, with additional help from fathers, brothers or cousins, plus the inevitable exposure to Django's recordings. Practise is intense and takes up a large part of daily life, with conventional schooling taking a secondary, and often non-existent, place in importance. Although the old gypsy way of life has to an extent been destroyed by the relentless advance of modern times, many of these musicians still live in caravans, although the more successful ones rent or buy houses in order to have a base from which to work.

The repertoire of the gypsies would seem to be more diverse than the average "western" guitarist, taking in French "musette" waltzes, classical pieces, Latin American tunes, themes of Russian and Eastern European origins and a liberal dose of out and out jazz (or more accurately, Gypsy jazz). Also the approach to the guitar, both mentally and physically, is quite different, involving a chordal system which can be traced directly back to Django, plus a way of embroidering and embellishment which springs from the gypsy "savoir faire", epitomised in Reinhardt's playing. Very few gypsies read music and some are completely illiterate but, in general, they have photographic memories and can assimilate elements of music and anything else around them at an extremely fast rate.

There are three main 'tribes' or families of gypsies on the Continent — Manouche, Gitane and Siniti, the last being found mainly in Germany. All speak the language of the country of their abode and, to a greater or lesser extent, the Romany tongue. Thus a gypsy from Hungary, say, can often communicate quite easily with one from France.

Bireli Lagrene

Bireli, born in 1966 near Strasbourg, started playing at the age of 4 and was playing jazz at 6. He is, without doubt, one of the most important players to date and has already built a formidable reputation in France, Germany and Switzerland. His father, Fiso, was a guitarist of some renown in France during the Thirties. Bireli plays with a ferocious swing and a risk-taking spontaneity that is very reminiscent of Django. Joseph Reinhardt has publicly stated that, "he's playing the way Django used to play", and, so the story goes, was reduced to tears when he first heard Bireli. Recently Bireli's style has become much more modern and he mostly plays an electric guitar with various effects pedals and, on occasion a guitar synthesiser.

Records

"Routes to Django" (recorded at 13)	Jazz Point 1003 (Germany) Re-issued on Island Records AN 1002
"Bireli Swing 81"	Jazz Point 1009
"Bireli Lagrene 15"	Antilles (Island Records) AN 1009
"Down in Town"	Antilles (Island Records) AN 1019
"Bireli Lagrene Ensemble — Live"	Jazz Point 1015

Lousson Reinhardt

Alias Henri Baumgartner, Lousson is Django's first son and played with Django's group in the late 40's. He plays mostly electric guitar in the mainstream jazz style. Lousson still lives the nomadic life, is rarely seen and, as far as is known, has not recorded since his father died.

Babik Reinhardt

Babik is Django's youngest son and a fine guitarist, with a couple of records to his credit. He has led a rather chequered career and was off the scene for many years. Happily, he is now performing and recording again, choosing to play electric guitar in the American style rather than copy his father.

Records (possibly unobtainable now): Sinti Houn Brazil French CBS 65635
Sur le Chemin de Mon Pere French
MFP 2M048-52026
Three Of A Kind. J.M.S.038
(with Boulou Ferré and
Christian Escoudé)
Excellent and recently available (1986)

Joseph Reinhardt

Sadly, Joseph Reinhardt passed away on February 24th, 1982, aged 70. Django's brother and principal rhythm player, he was the mainstay of the original Quintet 'back up' sound, and on the evidence of a few hard to obtain records, is a great soloist in his own right. Joseph lived in a caravan and was always on the move, still playing guitar up to his death but rarely in public after Django died. He is buried with Django at Samois-sur-Seine, near Fontainbleu, France.

Boulou and Elios Ferré

Probably the greatest duo in the history of the guitar, Boulou and his younger brother, Elios, make a formidable team. They are able to play virtually any piece of music in a dazzling variety of styles and, if fed intraveneously, could probably play for weeks without repeating themselves. Sons of Pierre 'Matelo' Ferré, the great and mysterious genius of the guitar, they have been drenched in music from an early age.

Boulou made his first concert appearance at the age of 9 and at 13 recorded an album of Charlie Parker tunes on which he is heard scat-singing along with his guitar lines. Since then he has gone from strength to strength, encompassing and mixing all kinds of music to form a style that is unique and extremely advanced in harmonic concept. Boulou has the ability to take the attentive listener into realms unknown, employing many gypsy devices in his playing to manipulate his audience onto a higher level of consciousness. He differs from the other guitarists in that he doesn't attempt to play like Django but prefers to extend Django's harmonic concept in mish-mash of forms that extend from medieval times through to and beyond the present.

Elios is never very far behind, backing his brother with a stunning mixture of bass runs, harmony lines and complex chords to the extent that it is often difficult to establish who is playing what. Elios also plays marvellous Flamenco guitar, sometimes accompanying his own singing. The brothers, occasionally joined by a third brother, Michel, tend to play in very exclusive restaurants in Paris and, in the Summer season, along the French Riviera. They also play at jazz concerts and make short tours to Switzerland and Germany etc.

Their father, Matelo, died on 24th January 1989, aged 70. Matelo had two brothers, Sarrane and Baro, who are now dead but were both brilliant guitarists, particularly Baro, whose memory is revered in the family, and who played rhythm on many of Django's records. Matelo also worked and recorded with Django, but to a lesser extent. All the family are prolific composers.

Records

Boulou and Elios Ferré "Pour Django"	Steeplechase SCS1120
Boulou and Elios Ferré "Gypsy Dreams"	Steeplechase SCS1140
Boulou and Elios Ferré "Trinity"	Steeplechase SCS1171
Boulou Ferré Quartet "Relax and Enjoy"	Steeplechase SCS1210
Baro Ferre	Hot Club Records HCD45
Matelo Ferre	Hot Club Records HCD46

Mondin and Ninin

Mondin is Ninin's father and is a Manouche gypsy, of the same tribe as Django. Both father and son are virtually illiterate and play in a crude, earthy style possessing great charm, usually appearing as a duo. They have made only one record on an obscure French label which they sell at their gigs which are mainly in the Flea Market in Paris.

They alternate with solo and rhythm work, both playing Maccaferri copies with fitted pick-ups through one cheap amplifier. Although some of the Django tunes and standard jazz pieces are played with odd bar lengths, father and son always change chord at exactly the same time and one cannot help but be enticed by their music.

Raphael Fays

Raphael was born in Paris in 1959 of Italian gypsy descent and like his idol, Django, is of the Manouche tribe who are renowned as musicians and craftsmen. He began playing at the age of twelve and was taught the basics by his father, Louis, who is a great guitarist in his own right. Raphael has spent many years studying Django's records and is able to play along with the records so closely that it is almost impossible on a tape replay to distinguish who is playing what. He possesses an incredible technique coupled with amazing speed and an endless repertoire. In between the essential functions of life, he plays incessantly so that the tips of his fingers are black and the neck of his Favino guitar is stripped down to the bare wood.

Like all the gypsies, Raphael goes for anything that's good in music from Bach to Charlie Parker and, in fact, is a tremendous bona fide classical guitarist, making many of the so called 'names' in this field seem tame by comparison. He makes a comfortable living from his music, touring all over the Continent, making records and T.V. appearances. He prefers to work in a trio context with a double bass and his father Louis on rhythm guitar. Louis is one of the finest rhythm players around with a unique chord system which often involves a running bass line. He is also one of the few gypsies who can read notation and, in general, has a vast knowledge of the guitar. Both father and son are remarkable composers in the jazz and classical idioms.

Suggested listening

"Night in Caravan"	W.E.A. 58232
"Bon Jour Gypsy"	W.E.A. 240103-1

Maurice Ferret

Maurice is a Gitane gypsy and a cousin of the great Pierre 'Matlo' Ferré who played rhythm with Django. He operates as a duo with another cousin, Joseph Pouville, playing the bars and cafes of Paris. They have recorded two albums to date on an obscure French label and always carry copies to sell at their gigs. Maurice uses a "D" hole Favino guitar with a Stimer pick-up similar to that used by Django after 1946. He is one of the finest exponents of the "tzigane" style and plays with tremendous flourish.

Fapy Lafertin

Fapy, now in his thirties, comes from Belgium and until recently was the main soloist with a quartet called Waso. Of all the gypsies he plays with the sweetest tone, uses a 'D' hole Maccaferri and gets very close to Django's melodic aspect. Possessing a beautiful fluid technique, he has the same continuity of chords and phrasing that Django had and often quotes Django's solos extending them with little frills of his own. Fapy is a versatile musician playing violin, mandolin, harp as well as guitar.

Waso, consisting essentially of bass, two guitars and clarinet/saxophone tour all the time and have made many trips to England. With Fapy their repertoire consisted mainly of Reinhardt material and swing standards, but they also included several Hungarian gypsy pieces with the rhythm guitarist switching to piano and vocals, Fapy on violin or mandolin and the reed player on guitar. This group still exists and often tours England. Fapy has recently formed his own quartet.

Waso "Live in Laren"	Polydor 2925111
Waso "Gypsy Swing Vol. 5"	Munich BM150246

Waso is due to have a record released on the American GHB label, featuring the new line-up.
Fapy Lafertin "Fapology"   Cassette available from: Dave Bennett, 1 Blackbird Close, Basingstoke, Hants.

Other gypsy jazz groups and guitarists, all fine players, abound throughout France and Germany, including the outfits Hans'che Weiss, La Romanderie The Sinti Hot Club and individualists such as Costa Lucas, Lulu Reinhardt, Schnuckenack Reinhardt.

Django's house at Samois Sur Seine

Maurice Ferret chats to Joseph Reinhardt: Samois 1978

Maurice Ferret & Joseph Pouville's double act: Montmartre 1978

LOUSSON REINHARDT
1978

Joseph Reinhardt 1978

BABIK REINHARDT
SAMOIS 1983

BOULOU & ELIOS FERRÉ
at Samois 1978 with Louis Vola (bass)
& Svend Asmussen.

Bireli Lagrene
rehearsing
London 1982

Gaiti Lagrene, Bireli's brother
& rhythm guitarist in original
group

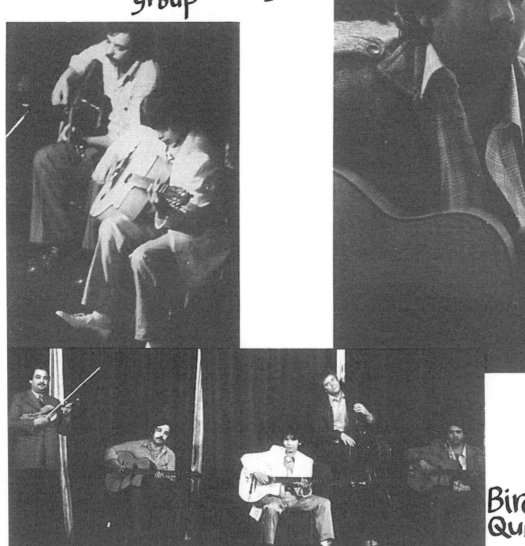

Bireli Lagrene
Quintet, London
1982

Boulou & Elios with Louis Vola &
Svend Asmussen, Samois 1978

↓BOULOU & ELIOS→

Pierre
'Matelo'
Ferré
Samois
1985

Boulou &
Elios
Pigalle, Paris
1980

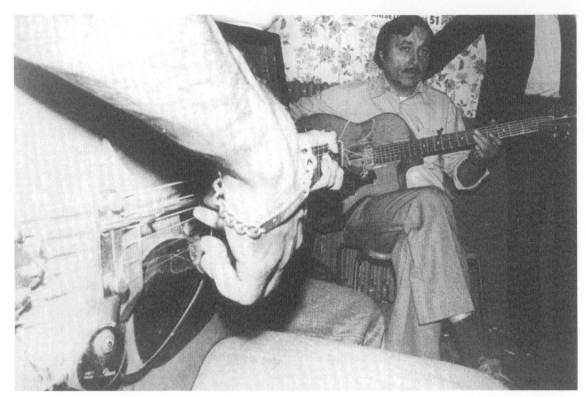

Mondin at 'La Chope' in the Fleamarket, Paris, 1980. Ninin in foreground.

Ninin's battered guitar complete with Stimer pickup

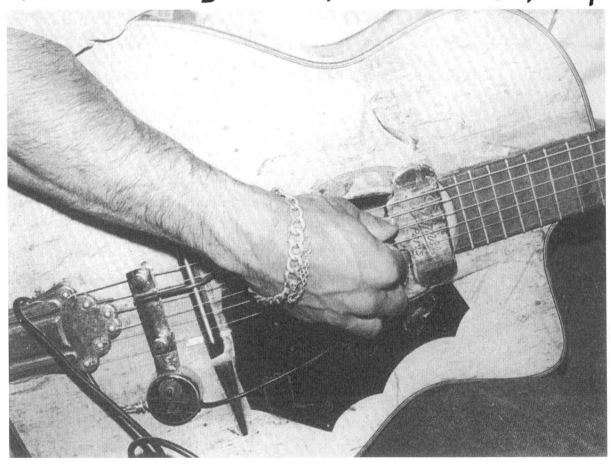

Christian Escoudé, Samois 1985

Tschirglo Loeffler, rhythm guitarist with Bireli's original group. London 1982

Maurice Ferret, Pigalle, Paris 1979

Bireli Lagrene London 1982

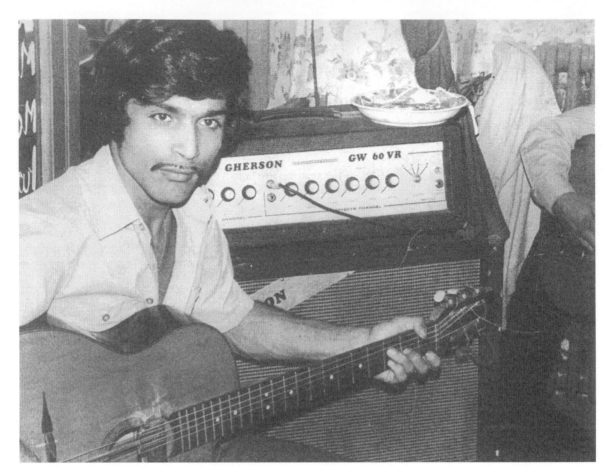

NININ

PARIS 1980

MONDIN

Raphael Fays ↑
← Louis Fays
Raphael Fays Trio, Samois 1978 ↓

Wedili Koeler
Violinist in Bireli's original
group & a fine guitarist
in his own right.

Louis Fays 1981

48